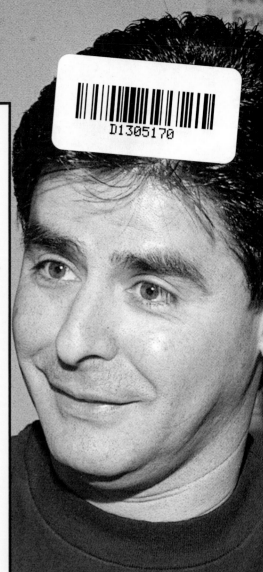

Call Mr. Vasquez, He'll Fix It!

Written by
ALICE K. FLANAGAN

Photographs by
CHRISTINE OSINSKI

Reading Consultant
LINDA CORNWELL
Learning Resource Consultant
Indiana Department Of Education

CHILDREN'S PRESS®   *A Division of Grolier Publishing*
New York • London • Hong Kong • Sydney • Danbury, Connecticut

Special thanks to Roberto Vasquez for allowing us to tell his story.

Library of Congress Cataloging-in-Publication Data
Flanagan, Alice K.
    Call Mr. Vasquez, he'll fix it! / by Alice K. Flanagan; photographs by Christine Osinski.
        p.   cm. — (Our neighborhood)
    Summary: Describes the work done each day by a Chilean American who is the building maintenance contractor responsible for a neighborhood apartment building.
    ISBN: 0-516-20045-3 (lib. bdg.)—0-516-26062-6 (pbk.)
    1. Apartment houses—Maintenance and repair—Juvenile literature. 2. Janitors—Juvenile literature. [1. Apartment houses—Maintenance and repair. 2. Occupations.] I. Osinski, Christine. ill. II. Title. III. Series: Our neighborhood (New York, N.Y.)
    TH3351.F58   1996
    647'.92'0288—dc20   96-17167
                                                                    CIP
                                                                    AC

Photographs ©: Christine Osinski

He unlocks the doors
and turns on the lights.

Mr. Vasquez, my neighbor, sometimes works day and night.

He's in charge of a building
that is sixteen floors high.

He's always on call
when something goes wrong.

A drain on the roof is blocked.

The walkway is icy.

 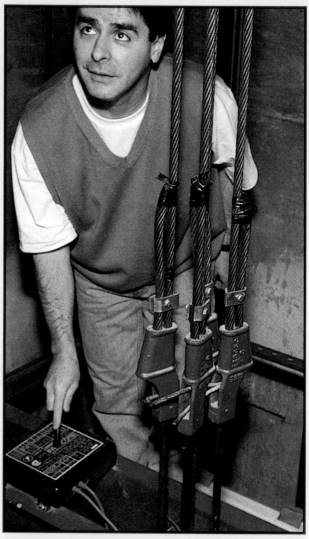

An elevator has stopped working.

The boiler needs fixing.

A water pipe has broken.

A light has gone out.

14

Get Mr. Vasquez,
the building maintenance contractor.

1

If he can't fix it, he knows
the right person to call.

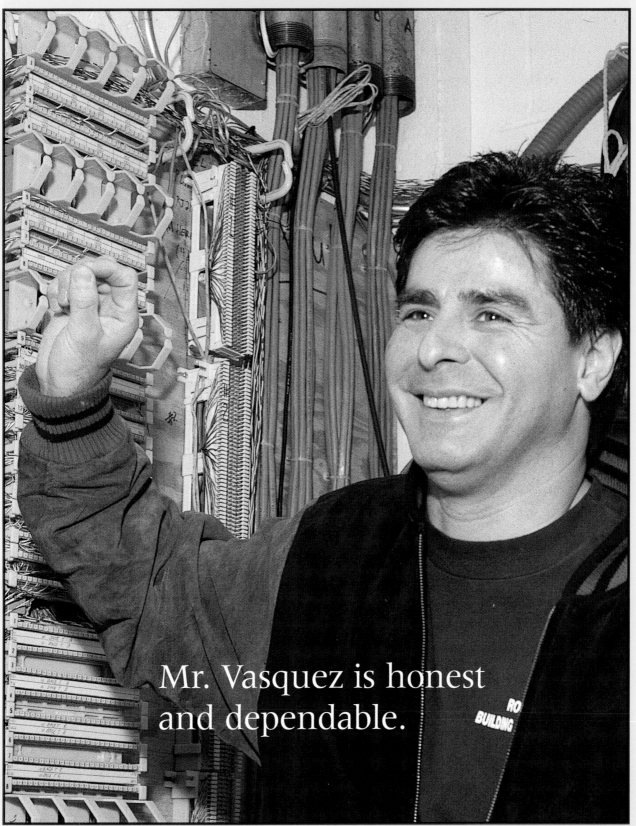

Mr. Vasquez is honest and dependable.

He keeps the building
in tip-top shape.

Eight people work with him
to keep it safe.

Each person has a duty —
to clean, paint, or repair.

They use portable radios
to keep in touch.

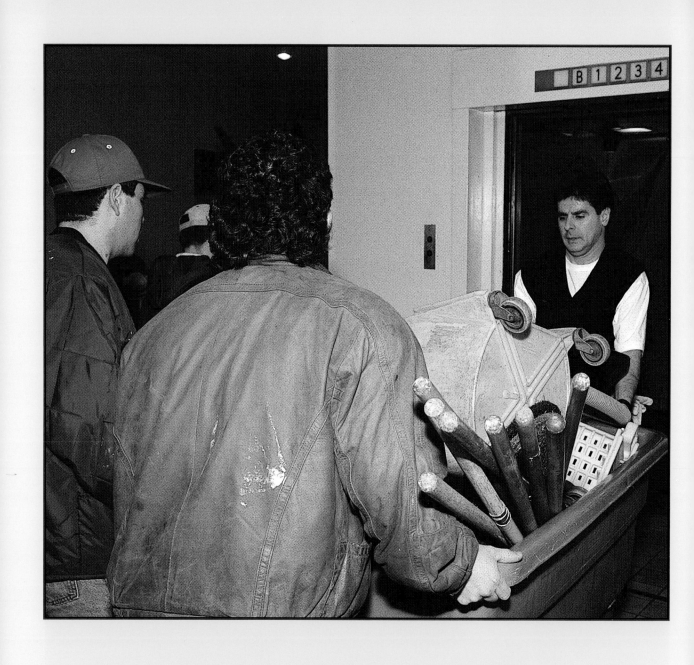

Mr. Vasquez shows the workers
how to work together

to solve any problem,
or to fix any machine.

At the end of the day, Mr. Vasquez checks their work to be sure that each person has done the job well.

He writes a report and then signs it.
Mr. Vasquez is responsible for
everything his workers do.

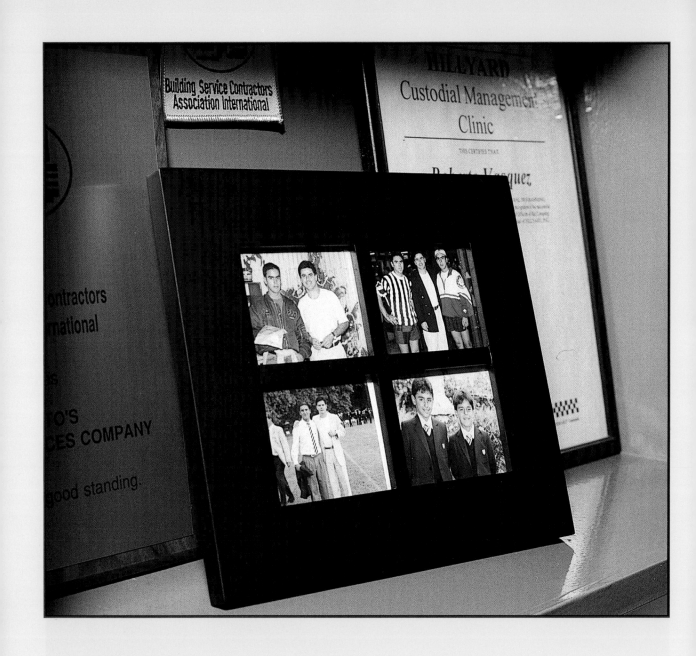

Mr. Vasquez came to America
fourteen years ago.

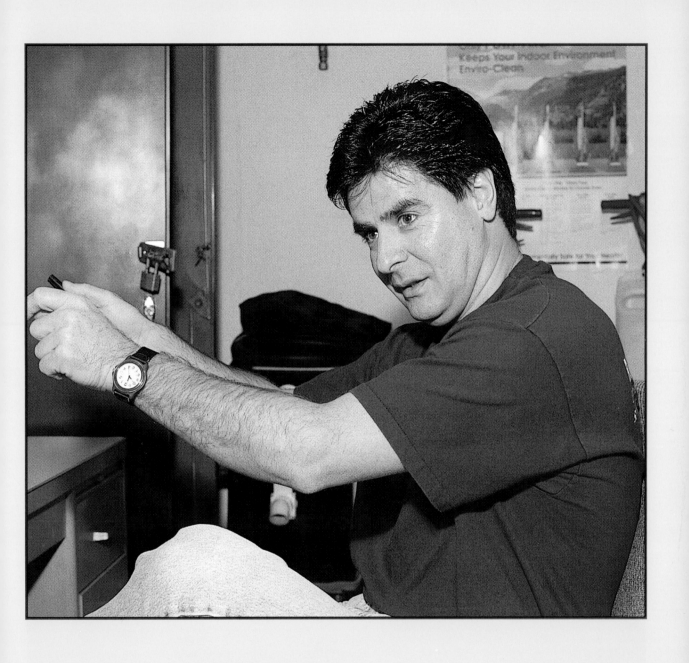

He left Chile to start
a business of his own.

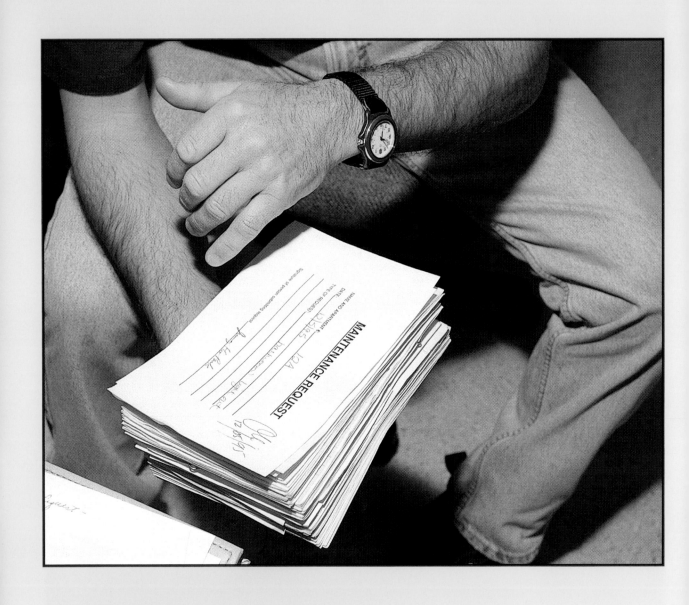

Now many people depend on him to keep their building safe and clean.

When they call him for a repair, they always hear him say, "No problem. I'll be right there to fix it for you!"

ROBERTO'
BUILDING MAINT

Meet the Author
and the Photographer

Alice Flanagan and Christine Osinski are sisters. They grew up together telling stories and drawing pictures in a brown brick bungalow in a southwest-side neighborhood of Chicago, Illinois. Today they write stories and take photographs professionally.

Ms. Flanagan resides in Chicago with her husband and works as a freelance writer. Ms. Osinski is a photographer and teaches at The Cooper Union for the Advancement of Science and Art in New York City. She lives with her husband and two sons on Staten Island.